The Hugging Sea

A Waverley Story Book for Children

Written by Amanda Stanford
Illustrated by Gemma Stuart

The Reworkd Press
Charlotte, 2014

For wee Evie

We walk down

by the sea.

I hug you and

you hug me.

Waves crash down and wind blows fast.

Out, out, fly our hugs to rush and swirl and dance.

Stretch your

arms wide,

wide, wide

So that around

the world and

back again

Our hugs return

From where they came down by the sea that day.

About the author:

Dr. Amanda Stanford earned her PhD in English Creative Writing from the University of Edinburgh. She has taught writing and English classes for seven years in the US, Mexico, Japan, and Egypt. She also writes historical fiction under the pen name A M Montes de Oca.

About the illustrator:

Gemma Stuart grew up near the sea in Edinburgh, Scotland. She has a degree in Illustration from Edinburgh College of Art and currently enjoys illustrating her own short stories. She participates in several local events, where she sells her art directly to the art-loving public.

www.ingramcontent.com/pod-product-compliance
Lightning Source LLC
Chambersburg PA
CBHW040022050426
42452CB00002B/101